SandCastle™

First Sounds

Gina and George

Kelly Doudna

Consulting Editor, Diane Craig, M.A./Reading Specialist

ABDO Publishing Company

Published by ABDO Publishing Company, 4940 Viking Drive, Edina, Minnesota 55435.

Printed in the United States.

Credits
Edited by: Pam Price
Curriculum Coordinator: Nancy Tuminelly
Cover and Interior Design and Production: Mighty Media
Child Photography: Steven Wewerka, Wewerka Photography
Photo Credits: Brand X Pictures, Comstock, Corbis Images, John Foxx, Photodisc

Library of Congress Cataloging-in-Publication Data

Doudna, Kelly, 1963-
    Gina and George / Kelly Doudna.
        p. cm. -- (First sounds)
    Includes index.
    ISBN 1-59679-156-X (hardcover)
    ISBN 1-59679-157-8 (paperback)
        1. English language--Consonants--Juvenile literature. I. Title. II. Series.
PE1159.D684 2005
428.1'3--dc22

                                                                    2004059231

SandCastle™ books are created by a professional team of educators, reading specialists, and content developers around five essential components that include phonemic awareness, phonics, vocabulary, text comprehension, and fluency. All books are written, reviewed, and leveled for guided reading, early intervention reading, and Accelerated Reader® programs and designed for use in shared, guided, and independent reading and writing activities to support a balanced approach to literacy instruction.

Let Us Know

After reading the book, SandCastle would like you to tell us your stories about reading. What is your favorite page? Was there something hard that you needed help with? Share the ups and downs of learning to read. We want to hear from you! To get posted on the ABDO Publishing Company Web site, send us e-mail at:

sandcastle@abdopub.com

SandCastle Level: Beginning

Gg

ABCDEFGH
IJKLMNOPQ
RSTUVWXYZ

abcdefgh
ijklmnopq
rstuvwxyz

Gina

George

giraffe

gingerbread

giant

general

gem

Here is a .

The is good.

The is big.

Here is a .

Here is a .

Gina and George like gingerbread.

The gingerbread
is good.

The giraffe likes gingerbread too.

Which of these pictures begin with g?

More words that begin with g

gee

generation

gentle

gerbil

germ

German

gesture

gym

About SandCastle™

A professional team of educators, reading specialists, and content developers created the SandCastle™ series to support young readers as they develop reading skills and strategies and increase their general knowledge. The SandCastle™ series has four levels that correspond to early literacy development in young children. The levels are provided to help teachers and parents select the appropriate books for young readers.

Emerging Readers
(no flags)

Beginning Readers
(1 flag)

Transitional Readers
(2 flags)

Fluent Readers
(3 flags)

These levels are meant only as a guide. All levels are subject to change.

To see a complete list of SandCastle™ books and other nonfiction titles from ABDO Publishing Company, visit www.abdopub.com or contact us at:
4940 Viking Drive, Edina, Minnesota 55435 • 1-800-800-1312 • fax: 1-952-831-1632